Ben & Holly's Little Kingdom

The Little Forest

Elf Oak Wood

Gaston's Cave

Elf Windmill

Elf Farm

Little Castle

The Meadow

Great Elf Tree

Mrs Witch's House

Frog Pond

N W E S

Royal Golf Course

The Bramble Woods

The Pine Forest

Gaston's Messy Cave

Today's adventure starts at Gaston's Cave . . .

Ben Elf and Princess Holly are visiting Gaston the Ladybird.
"Are you coming out to play, Gaston?" asks Holly.
"Woof, woof!" barks Gaston. He loves playing
with Ben and Holly.

"Hee, hee, hee!" giggles Holly, flying off. "I bet you two can't catch me!"

"Yes we can!" cries Ben, jumping onto Gaston's back. "Come on, Gaston, giddy-up!"

Buzzzzzzzzzz! Gaston and Ben zoom off after Holly.

The three friends are having lots of fun playing in the Meadow.
"Gaston loves fetching sticks," says Ben. "Gaston! Fetch!"
"Woof, woof!" barks Gaston the Ladybird, running after a stick
and bringing it back, happily.
"Well done, Gaston!" cheers Ben.
"Clever Gaston!" adds Princess Holly.

"Woof!" barks Gaston, as Ben and Holly
roll him onto his back to wiggle his legs.
Suddenly, they hear a familiar voice calling,
"Holly! Bedtime!"

6

"That's Nanny Plum," cries Holly. "I've got to go home now. Bye, Ben! Bye, Gaston!"
"Oh! We were having such fun," sighs Ben.
"Never mind. We'll meet up again tomorrow," smiles Holly, happily.

Just then, Ben hears Mrs Elf shout to him, "Ben! Bedtime!"
"Oh, that's my mum!" says Ben. "I'd better be off. Goodbye,
Gaston. See you tomorrow."
"Woof!" barks Gaston.
Gaston is very tired, so he goes to bed too. His bed is inside
his cave. It is very messy and very smelly, but Gaston likes
it and soon falls asleep.

The next morning, Ben and Holly go to Gaston's cave, but he isn't there. "Maybe Gaston's sad and that's why he won't play with us," says Princess Holly. "Maybe he doesn't like us riding on him and tipping him on his back," says Ben.

Gaston

Holly tells Nanny Plum that Gaston the
Ladybird is sad and she comes to help.
"No wonder Gaston is sad. No one could be happy
in such a messy, smelly cave," says Nanny Plum.
"Chop, chop! We must clean it up!"

Nanny Plum waves her wand and says the magic words to help with the cleaning.
"Abracadee Abracadop!
Brushes Dusters Soap and Mop!"
Suddenly, lots of lovely cleaning things appear.

"Holly, you dust the cobwebs," says Nanny Plum. "Ben, you clean the floor and I'll tackle the bed."
"Yes, Nanny Plum," cry Ben and Holly.

13

"This bed is filthy!" cries Nanny Plum.
"Old food, lollipops and smelly socks! Eugh!"
Nanny waves her wand again.
"Bish Bash Besh!
Gaston's Bed Nice and Fresh!"

ZING! Now Gaston has a lovely clean bed to sleep in. "Just a final polish and we're done!" says Nanny Plum, using her magic to make everything sparkly. "Ooooh!" gasp Ben and Holly.

Just then, Gaston arrives, but he doesn't look sad at all.
Ben and Holly tell him they are sorry for rolling him over and riding
on his back. But Gaston says he isn't sad.
Just then, Gaston sees his new shiny clean cave and bursts into tears.
"Sob! Sob!" Oh dear! *Now* Gaston is sad. "Woof! Woof!"
"He said he loved his home just as it was," translates Nanny Plum.
"All messy and smelly!"

"Oh! Sorry, Gaston," cries Princess Holly. "We thought you needed cheering up."

"Don't worry," says Ben. "We'll make your cave just the way you like it!"

"We're very good at making things messy!" giggles Holly. Ben and Holly start adding cobwebs to the walls and making the cave as messy and smelly as they can!

Nanny Plum uses a spell on Gaston's bed.
"Zip Zap Zessy! Gaston's Cave Nice and Messy!"

Gaston

Gaston is so happy, he jumps into his marvellously messy bed.

"Let's add smelly socks!" cries Holly.

"And lollipops!" cheers Ben Elf.

Finally, Nanny Plum adds a lovely layer of dirt over the whole cave.

WOOF!
WOOF!

"Well done, everybody!" smiles Nanny Plum.
"That smells just as bad as it did before!"
"Hooray!" cheer Ben and Holly together.

Gast

"Woof! Woof!" barks Gaston, happily.
"If you ever want us to make your cave untidy again, Gaston," cries Holly. "Don't be afraid to ask."
"Yes," adds Ben. "That's what friends are for."

See you soon!